# Twenty to M...

# Mini Mosaics

## Aimee Harman

Search Press

First published in Great Britain 2015

Search Press Limited
Wellwood, North Farm Road,
Tunbridge Wells, Kent TN2 3DR

Text copyright © Aimee Harman 2015

Photographs by Simon Pask

Photographs and design copyright
© Search Press Ltd 2015

Print ISBN: 978-1-78221-110-5
ebook ISBN: 978-1-78126-241-2

**Suppliers**
If you have difficulty in obtaining any of the
materials and equipment mentioned in this book,
then please visit the Search Press website for
details of suppliers: www.searchpress.com

Printed in China

## Dedication

*I would like to dedicate this book to my late
husband, Mark, and to Gabrielle, my sister;
may they both rest in peace.*

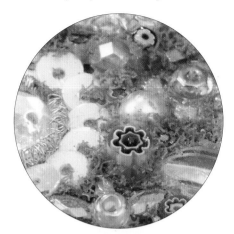

# Contents

# Introduction

This collection of mosaic projects is perfect for those who want to dip their toe in the water, and those with some experience of making mosaics. I like to experiment with mixed media to inspire my students, as I believe that mosaics do not always have to be restricted to the use of tiles alone.

Although I studied at art college, I have realised that you do not have to be an artist to create a mosaic; with the right tools and materials, you can create a design for a beautiful mirror, a coaster set, a wall hanging or a piece of jewellery. You can trace the outline of a design you like, draw your own design, or stick down a photocopy and apply mosaic tiles straight on top. I believe that practice and not being afraid to experiment are the best ways to improve and find your own unique style.

I have always believed that the skill involved in any mosaic is how you cut the tiles and place them in a way that gives the design flow and movement – called *andemento* in Italian. It is not about how good an artist you are, but about being willing to challenge yourself and believing you can do anything in mosaic-making. Once you have the basic tools and know-how, the sky's the limit.

Mosaics are so versatile and can be installed inside or outside to create a beautiful environment in any location, as long as the correct adhesives and methods are used. The process of making a mosaic is very absorbing – and the feeling you get when you clean off the grout, stand back and look at your finished piece is indescribable, knowing that your creation will be around for many many years to come.

There should be a warning with this subject, though – it can become highly addictive and you will often end up with half a cup of cold tea and some very late nights!

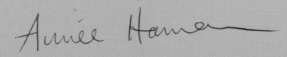

4

# Tools and materials

**Tile nippers** are essential for cutting vitreous glass, smalti, mirror and ceramic tiles. Ordinary ones cut with a pincer movement, while **wheeled tile nippers**, such as those made by Leponitt, have two cutting wheels and tend to be a little more accurate.

**MDF board** is an ideal base for mosaics for indoor use. It is hard, inexpensive and relatively easy to cut, but use a protective **face mask** if you are doing it yourself and do not breath in the dust.

**Rubber gloves** It is a good idea to wear these, as well as a protective face mask, when grouting your mosaic, as grout can be a skin irritant.

**Safety goggles** are an essential item for all tile cutting, especially when using glass and mirrors.

A small **paintbrush** is useful for painting MDF boards and applying glue to the MDF base.

**Pencil and tracing paper** Use these to copy your designs onto MDF boards or other surfaces.

A **sponge** is used to apply grout to a mosaic, and also to clean excess grout off the surface.

**Tweezers** and **cocktail sticks** are useful tools to help position tiles and other items on a mosaic.

**Impregnating sealer**, available from DIY stores, is useful for sealing marble and ceramic tiles to protect them and enrich the colours.

**Smalti** is made from slabs of handmade opaque glass. It is very uneven, which gives it a wonderful reflective quality, and comes in lovely, rich colours. **Vitreous glass tiles** are the same depth, so are particularly useful for projects requiring flat surfaces.

**Millefiori** are very decorative, cylindrical pieces of glass with central flower patterns and are used as occasional accents in a design. **Marble tiles** come in muted, natural shades and can be used for indoor or outdoor projects. **Tesserae** is another name for tiles (the singular is **tessera**).

**PVA glue** is a white adhesive that dries clear, and is strong enough to hold down tiles until they are ready to grout. **Epoxy adhesive** is very strong and useful for sticking a picture hanger to a heavy mosaic, for example. **Silicone adhesive** is useful for gluing mosaic tiles to ceramic surfaces, as they are less likely to slide around.

**Grout** is a cement-based powder that is mixed with water to make a paste and used to fill the gaps between tiles. This strengthens the mosaic and also serves to complete the design, as the gaps, if left, can be a distraction. Always follow the manufacturer's instructions.

**Varnish** is a useful sealant to protect outdoor projects, and to enhance the colour of mosaic tiles.

**Craft sprinkles** such as Flower Soft® moss are useful for creating the illusion of moss or grass and for backgrounds generally.

**Glitter sand** is a great way of creating a textured, sparkly background to a design.

**Acrylic paint** can be used for mosaic backgrounds if the whole thing is not to be covered in tiles.

**Masking tape** can be used to protect areas from getting covered in grout.

1 Tile nippers
2 Sponge
3 Paintbrush
4 Rubber gloves
5 Smalti
6 Ceramic tiles
7 Millefiori
8 Grout
9 MDF board
10 PVA glue

# Techniques

I have used basic mosaic techniques to make the projects in this book, so if you are a beginner you will find it very easy to follow, and if you are a more advanced mosaicist, you will hopefully find some inspiration among the mosaic designs here.

## Mosaic bases

You can create mosaics on many surfaces, such as wood, ceramic, concrete, metal and MDF. Here I have used mainly MDF, as this is an ideal material, being cheap to buy and easy to cut into your preferred shape. There are two main methods of mosaic: the direct and the indirect methods.

## The direct method

The direct method is the one I have used throughout this book, as it is the best one to use when you want a fast result. It is done by gluing mosaic tiles the right way up directly onto your chosen surface with adhesive, and then grouting the design once it is dry.

## The indirect method

The indirect, or reverse method involves creating your mosaic upside down on a sheet of paper or mesh. This is the best way to get a smooth, even finish which can be applied to most surfaces. Its great advantage is that it can be made away from the site, and installed when convenient. This is a method to try once you have some experience with the direct method.

## Grouting your work

The function of grout is twofold: to strengthen your mosaic by filling in all the gaps between the tiles and levelling the surface of the design, and to unify the appearance. It is the part that can make or break a mosaic. I tend to use dark grout in my work, as it looks more dramatic and really brings out the colours. It is best to avoid white as it does not give depth, but can look rather conspicuous, taking the focus away from the design.

Grout is the key to keeping a mosaic together in the strongest possible way. Without it, we would know much less than we do about ancient history, as grout has held Greek and Roman mosaics together for thousands of years, allowing us to learn from the techniques and designs of ancient mosaic artists.

Some mosaics, such as those made with smalti, are difficult to grout because of the varying heights of the tiles. They are sometimes made by placing the tiles closer together and not grouting at all.

## Design

Inspiration for designs can come from anywhere: a view, a colour, an image, or a feeling. Your job is to translate it into a unique piece of mosaic art. A design can be drawn straight onto your board, or some paper; or if you are not confident with drawing the design yourself, you can trace the image. Photocopying is useful if you want to enlarge or reduce the size of a design.

Alternatively, you can glue the image down onto the board and mosaic over it. This allows you to compare the colours in the design with your own tiles, and also to position your tiles more accurately.

## Mixed media

If you are not a purist, you may wish to use mixed media products such as beads, sequins, gems, broken china, feathers and glass nuggets. You can also personalise your designs further by adding fabric from items of clothing that have some sentimental value to you, or anything else that will adhere easily and complement your design.

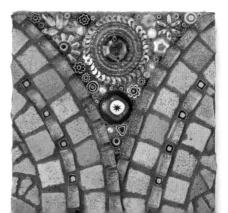

# Butterfly Paperweight

## Materials:

Large pebble

Ceramic tiles in beige, pale brown and shades of blue

Grey smalti

Millefiori

PVA glue

Black grout

Marble impregnating sealer (optional)

## Tools:

Tile nippers

Safety goggles

Paintbrush

Cocktail stick

Masking tape

Pencil or chalk

Masking tape

## Instructions:

**1** Find a fairly large, smooth-surfaced pebble; the flatter the better, as it will be easier to apply the mosaic tiles.

**2** Photocopy the template, then trace and transfer the design onto the pebble with a pencil, or chalk if the stone is a dark colour. Alternatively, you can cut it out and glue it onto the stone, making sure the whole area is stuck down. If the underside of the pebble is quite rounded, prop it up with pieces of tile to level it, so you can work flat.

**3** Using the tile nippers, cut the smalti and ceramic tiles into small pieces. Try to shape them so that they fit fairly neatly together, but do not worry too much about gaps, as these will be covered by the grout.

**4** Paint some glue onto the design using a fine paintbrush, and begin sticking on the tiles, starting at the edge of a wing. As the stone is porous, it will absorb the glue quite well and dry fairly quickly. Make sure you place the millefiori symmetrically in each wing, and try to place the tiles in flowing lines.

**5** Once the design is complete, leave to dry for at least three hours or overnight before grouting.

**6** Mix up the grout according to the manufacturer's instructions. I have used black grout to blend in with the colour of the pebble. Use masking tape to cover the pebble round the edge of the design to avoid getting grout all over the pebble. Apply the grout carefully over the butterfly design, filling all the gaps.

**7** Clean it up with a damp sponge and allow the grout a few hours to dry. Then buff it with a dry cloth. If you want to seal it, use a marble impregnating sealer to enrich the colours.

*Butterfly template: 100 per cent*

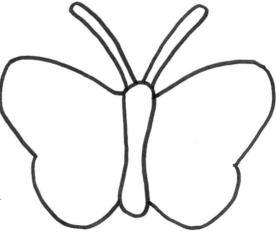

# Heart Brooch

## Materials:

Polymer modelling clay

Beads

Ceramic backing tiles in
assorted colours

Wire

Bead trimmings

Flat-backed crystals, semi-
precious stones and sequins

Tiles

Matt varnish

Epoxy adhesive

Brooch backs

## Tools:

Small rolling pin

Heart-shaped cutter

Craft knife

Cocktail stick

2 x flat-nosed pliers

Oven

Baking tray

Printer paper

## Instructions:

**1** Roll out the modelling clay to a depth of about 4mm (³/₁₆in).

**2** Using the heart-shaped cutter, cut out as many hearts as you can in the same batch and put them onto some printer paper to work on.

**3** Take the cocktail stick and apply the little gems, sequins and tiles by pushing them into the soft modelling clay, not too deep, in the pattern of your choice within the heart shape.

**4** To make the wire swirls, cut the wire into a 2.5cm (1in) length with some pliers and hold on to one end with the other pair of pliers. Twist it into a swirl and stick it down into the soft modelling clay.

**5** Once all the hearts are decorated, put them into the oven on a baking tray and follow the package instructions for baking the clay.

**6** Remove the hearts from the oven and leave to cool completely.

**7** Take a selection of the matt ceramic tiles and, using the epoxy adhesive, follow the instructions to stick the hearts straight onto the tiles, which act as the base of the brooches.

**8** When dry, turn the mosaic over and glue the brooch back onto the backing tile with the epoxy adhesive. Leave a space below to stick on some bead trimmings or a decoration of your choice.

**9** Leave until the glue is set.

# Flowerpot Bouquet

## Materials:

MDF board approx.
 7 x 7cm (2¾ x 2¾in)

Mini tiles

Flat-backed gems

Millefiori

Sequins

Beads

Trims

Pearl, glass and seed beads

Green craft sprinkles

Glitter sand

Strong magnet

PVA glue

## Tools:

Paintbrush

Cocktail stick

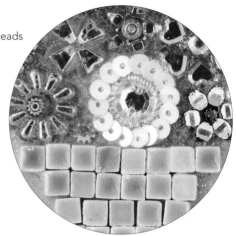

## Instructions:

**1** Start by placing the mini tiles in the shape of the pot on the board. When you are happy with the shape, dab some glue under each tile with the paintbrush, one by one, and put them back in place on the board.

**2** Next, place the flowers on the board and arrange them to fit in the area above the pot. Once you like the arrangement, take them off in the pattern you have made and place next to the board.

**3** Apply glue with the paintbrush above the pot wherever the flowers are going to be positioned. Leave a little space at the sides to show the background, and to give the flowers more height than width.

**4** Start sticking the flower gems, beads, millefiori and sequins into the wet glue, leaving little spaces in between them all.

**5** Now sprinkle the green craft moss into the gaps and use a cocktail stick to push the moss into the glue, ensuring it is stuck down firmly.

**6** Paint the remaining background of the board with the glue, and sprinkle the

glitter sand all over it, right up to the edge of the flowers and the pot.

**7** When it is dry, paint glue over the sides of the board and sprinkle glitter sand on them to give a nice finish.

**8** Once it has dried, turn the design over and stick on a strong magnet with a generous dab of glue. Leave it to dry for at least an hour before using.

# Tea, Darling?

## Materials:

Wooden teacup-shaped base

PVA glue

Pieces of pretty broken china

Pearl beads

Heart-shaped gem and flat-
 backed beads or gems

Glitter sand

Paint

## Tools:

Tile nippers

Safety goggles

Paintbrush

Strong magnet

Plastic bag

## Instructions:

**1** Paint the wooden base of the teacup in a colour of your choice to hide the wood, as this project will not be grouted. Allow it to dry.

**2** Using the tile nippers, start to cut up the broken china. This can be done safely within a plastic bag so all the pieces stay inside the bag. There will be some curved bits of china, if you are using bowls and cups, but by making them smaller, the curves lessen and the pieces will be flatter and easier to use as mosaic tiles.

**3** Once you have a selection of flat pieces of china, you can start laying them on the board to see how they fit together. If you are using a heart-shaped gem, place it near the centre. Once you are happy that you have a good design, you can

fill in any gaps with little pearl or plastic beads, or any other embellishments you wish to use, to add some variety to the project.

**4** Carefully remove the pieces of china you have laid out and try to keep them in order next to the base.

**5** Using the paintbrush, apply some glue to the whole of the base. You can be generous with the glue, as it dries clear, so it is not a problem if it gets on the china.

**6** Add the china pieces to the glued base, leaving some little spaces between the china for the glitter sand. Add the pearl beads and anything else you are using, and finish the handle with some flat-backed beads or gems.

**7** Sprinkle the glitter sand over the whole project and gently tap it so it falls in all the gaps. Leave it to dry for an hour or so, then shake off the excess. If you do not want to add glitter sand, place the china pieces and beads closer together with fewer gaps.

**8** Once it has dried, turn the design over and stick on a strong magnet with a generous dab of glue. Leave it to dry for at least an hour before using.

**Note:** This project can also be grouted as an alternative way of finishing the design, but it will not have a smooth finish as china tends to be rather bumpy and sharp.

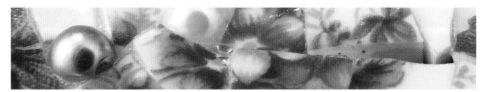

# Roman Coaster

## Materials:
MDF board approx.
  9 x 9cm (3½ x 3½in)
Marble tesserae
Black gravel sand
Replica Roman coin
PVA glue
Paper
Grout (optional)

## Tools:
Paintbrush
Cocktail stick
Black paint
Pencil

## Instructions:

**1** Place the Roman coin in the centre of the board and draw around it with a pencil.

**2** Lay out the marble tesserae on the board in a design of your choice, making a pleasing geometric pattern, and leave little gaps between the tiles. There should be an obvious mistake made within the mosaic, such as the wrong colour in a sequence. This was traditionally done because the Romans were superstitious and felt if they made a mistake it would please the gods, as it showed they were not perfect like them.

**3** Once you have decided on the design and are happy with it, carefully place the tiles next to the base in order.

**4** Using the paintbrush, apply glue over the board in a generous manner but avoid the edges. Then stick the tiles onto the board, leaving gaps in between.

**5** Sprinkle the gravel sand all over the mosaic, so that it lands in the wet glue in the gaps. Leave it to dry for an hour.

**6** Shake off the excess gravel sand and paint the edges of the board black.

**Note:** This project can also be grouted if you prefer. Follow the manufacturer's instructions, but avoid covering the coin in the middle, as it lies below the level of the marble tiles. It could also be used as a wall hanging by attaching a picture hook to the back.

# Child's Hand Panel

## Materials:

MDF board
Paint
Glue
Vintage fabric pieces
Lace cut-offs
Tassel trims
Smalti
Millefiori
Beads
Glass soft-edged nuggets
Flat-backed gems

Trimmings
Sequins
Black glitter sand
Sturdy picture hooks
Ribbon

## Tools:

Scissors
Tile nippers
Safety goggles
Paintbrush
Cocktail stick
Pencil

## Instructions:

**1** Draw around your child's hand on a piece of board about 10 x 10cm (4 x 4in).

**2** Using the scissors, cut up any old pieces of fabric that may have a significance to your child, such as clothing that is now too small or was worn for a special occasion.

**3** Apply the glue to the tips of the fingers first and create your preferred design with a mixture of smalti, beads and fabrics.

**4** Make each finger unique by gluing the fabric first as the base, and apply smalti, beads and gems with the cocktail stick, following the shape of each finger. Do this with each one and work your way down the hand to the wrist with the same technique, making each finger a different colour, but aiming to make those colours blend into each other.

**5** Make sure you have covered the whole hand with material so there are no gaps showing the board beneath, and leave it to dry for a few hours. The glue dries clear so it will not show if a little gets onto the beads or fabric.

**6** Once the hand is properly dry, paint the background blue, or a colour of your choice, then leave it to dry again. Then paint the background evenly with glue and sprinkle glitter sand all over the glue quite thickly so it absorbs. I used black over the blue to give it depth. Repeat this with the edges of the board once the top is dry.

**7** Add small but sturdy hooks to the top of the board, attach a ribbon, and hang.

# Stone Candle Holder

## Materials:

Broken piece of
  paving stone
PVA glue
Tea light
Mirror ball or mirror pieces
Ceramic tiles
Grout

## Tools:

Tile nippers
Safety goggles
Cocktail stick
Paintbrush
Pencil

## Instructions:

**1** Place the tea light in the centre of the broken paving stone and draw around it with a pencil. This will be the focal point of the design.

**2** Mirrors are a lovely medium to use for light reflection on this small scale. Use an old mirror ball and pick off the little pre-cut mirrors – that way there is no risk of shards flying around when cutting. Alternatively, you can use wheeled tile nippers to cut precise mirror squares, but you must wear safety goggles. Cut the ceramic tiles to shape before placing any down.

**3** To make the design, draw some curvy lines or swirls around the tea light circle with your pencil. Then, using the paintbrush, apply a generous amount of glue over the surface of the stone.

**4** Following the lines and swirls, place the tiles neatly in flowing shapes and fairly close together, but leave some space between the tiles and mirror pieces for the grout. The aim is to get the stone to resemble an ancient design on part of a broken mosaic floor. A border in one colour, or two contrasting colours using

the ceramic tiles, will help to achieve this effect (see above and right).

**5** Leave it to dry, and then grout according to the manufacturer's instructions. Be careful when grouting mirror, as the fine sand in the grout can scratch the mirror's surface; the finer the grade of the grout, the better.

**Note:** If you do not want to break the design with a circular gap for the holder, you can make a continuous design and simply place the tea light on top of the finished mosaic.

# Beetle Paperweight

## Materials:

Large pebble

Black ceramic tiles

Gold smalti

Coloured smalti

Millefiori

PVA glue

Grout

Marble impregnating
   sealer (optional)

## Tools:

Tile nippers

Safety goggles

Paintbrush

Cocktail stick

Masking tape

Pencil or chalk

## Instructions:

**1** Find a fairly large, smooth-surfaced pebble; the flatter the better, as it will be easier to apply the mosaic tiles.

**2** Photocopy the template, then trace and transfer the design onto the pebble with a pencil, or chalk if the stone is a dark colour. Alternatively, cut it out and glue it onto the stone, making sure the whole area is stuck down. If the underside of the pebble is quite rounded, prop it up with pieces of tile to level it, so you can work flat.

**3** Using the tile nippers, cut the smalti and ceramic tiles into small pieces. Try to shape them so that they fit fairly neatly together, but do not worry too much about gaps, as these will be covered by the grout.

**4** Paint some glue onto the design on the pebble using a fine paintbrush, and begin sticking on the tiles, starting at the edge of the beetle's

body. As the stone is porous, it will absorb the glue quite well and dry fairly quickly. Place the coloured smalti round the edge of the body, and the piece of gold smalti somewhere in the middle, to reflect the light.

**5** Once the design is complete, leave it to dry for at least three hours or overnight before grouting.

**6** Mix up the grout according to the manufacturer's instructions. Use masking tape to cover the pebble all round the edge of the mosaic design to avoid getting grout all over the pebble. Apply the grout carefully over the beetle design, filling all the gaps.

**7** Clean it up with a damp sponge, then buff with a dry cloth. Allow the grout a few hours to dry. If you want to seal it, use a marble impregnating sealer to enrich the colours.

*Beetle template:
100 per cent*

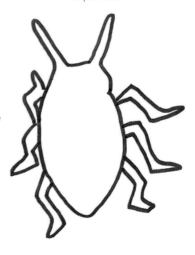

22

# Forget-me-not Heart

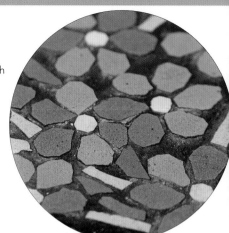

## Materials:

MDF board approx. 12.5 x 12.5cm (5 x 5in)

Blue, yellow and green ceramic tiles

PVA glue

Black glitter

Black sand

Black grout

Black paint

Images of forget-me-not flowers

Heart template

Matt or satin varnish

## Tools:

Tile nippers

Safety goggles

Paintbrush

Cocktail stick

Pencil

## Instructions:

**1** Draw around the heart template onto the middle of the board using the pencil.

**2** Using the nippers, cut up the blue tiles into small squares of about 5mm (¼in).

**3** Nip and shape the squares to round them, leaving one end slightly pointed to create the flower petal.

**4** Cut some smaller squares in yellow for the flower centres and make them into tiny circles by nipping off all the edges. Cut some slivers of green to make stems. Use the images for inspiration for your design.

**5** Lay out the flowers within the design so they all come up level with the edge of the heart shape. Once you are happy with the design, pick up each petal and start gluing down onto the board, filling in any spaces with green slivers to represent stems. Make sure you have left gaps in between for the grout.

**6** Leave the design to dry.

**7** Mix up the grout according to the manufacturer's instructions and grout the design, wiping off any excess. Leave to dry.

**8** Paint the background board black all the way around the outside of the heart.

**9** Once the paint has dried, cover with a thin layer of glue and immediately sprinkle a mixture of black sand and black glitter onto it, shaking off the excess.

**10** Once it has dried, varnish the heart mosaic area only with a matt or satin varnish.

Heart template:
enlarge to 200%

# Pink Choker

## Materials:

MDF board 2.5 x 2.5cm (1 x 1in)

Glue

Black grout

Stained glass pieces

Ceramic tiles

Mirror pieces

Glass beads

Glass tiles

Strong cotton thread

Crimp beads

Necklace clasp

## Tools:

Tile nippers

Safety goggles

Cocktail stick

Scissors

Fine sewing needle

Paintbrush

Flat-nosed pliers

Sponge

Paper towel

## Instructions:

**1** Cut six long pieces of thread to about 30.5cm (12in).

**2** Using the paintbrush, spread the glue over the whole area of the tiny 2.5 x 2.5cm (1 x 1in) board and lay three pieces of the thread across the board horizontally, so it is of equal length from left to right; this will be for making the beaded necklace part around the neck.

**3** Now lay three pieces of thread equally down the centre from the top of the square, but do not allow it to protrude over the top.

**4** Cut up all the tiles, glass and ceramic, with the tile cutters, using safety goggles.

**5** Apply more glue over the threads and add the tiles and mirror pieces, gluing them straight on top of the threads and leaving gaps in between for the grout and tiny seed

beads. Keep going until you have filled the square with a pleasing design.

**6** Leave to dry for an hour.

**7** Make up the grout according to the manufacturer's instructions. Apply the grout all over the mosaic, wiping off the excess while the grout is still wet. Push the tiny seed beads into the spaces between the tiles with the cocktail stick. Leave it to dry for an hour.

**8** Clean up the mosaic with a damp sponge, then dry it with a paper towel. It is now ready to bead.

**9** Thread a fine sewing needle onto the end of one of the horizontal threads of the necklace and fill with silver seed beads to the length required. Repeat this five times. Tie a knot at each end, then join the three strands

together and attach the necklace clasp according to the maker's instructions.

**10** For the three beaded dangles below the mosaic square, thread a fine sewing needle through the cotton and start making up a sequence design with the beads, combining larger and smaller beads. When you reach the bottom of the thread, tie it in a knot as tightly as you can and use glue on the knot to harden it. Using the flat-nosed pliers, cover the knot with a crimp bead to secure it.

**11** When the necklace is fully beaded, apply some glue to the outside edge of the mosaic. This seals the grout and stops it coming off on your skin or clothes. Paint the base of the tile black.

# Garden Mirror

## Materials:

MDF board approx. 7 x 7cm (2¾ x 2¾in)

Mirror square

Millefiori

Mini ceramic mosaic tiles or mini pebbles

PVA glue

Beads

Trims

Flat-backed gems

Gold fabric leaves

Sequins

Glitter sand

Paint

Magnet or picture hook

## Tools:

Paintbrush

Cocktail stick

## Instructions:

**1** First paint the MDF board with your chosen colour and leave it to dry.

**2** Place the mirror in the centre of the board and use the glue to stick it down.

**3** As mirrors can have sharp edges, start by making a frame with materials that will level up with the edges of the mirror. There are acrylic mirrors that are safer to use, but they tend to scratch very easily. Apply some glue, then stick down the small square tiles or the mini pebbles around the edge of the mirror in a pattern and sprinkle the glitter sand in the gaps. Use the cocktail stick to place everything so it is positioned neatly around the inner frame.

**4** The main frame of the mosaic is very easy and fun to do. Choose a pattern with the tiny beads and gold fabric leaves, adding accents and detail with the gems and millefiori. Alternatively, you could make your design more abstract and place the flower gems around the edge of the border. Lay out the design first so you know it will all fit. Then, working on one side of the board at a time, remove the pieces, apply glue to the board and stick them down.

**5** Once everything is glued down, sprinkle the glitter sand in the remaining gaps to fill the spaces between the flowers. If you prefer the painted board effect, do not use the glitter sand. A dark base colour shows the design up better.

**6** Once it is dried, stick a magnet to the back with glue. Alternatively, add a picture hook and the mirror is ready to hang.

# Leaf Tile

## Materials:
Skeleton leaves
Polymer modelling clay
Seed beads
Crystal beads
Mirror pieces
Millefiori
Silver wire
Tiles
Flat-backed crystals
Small bathroom tile
Picture hook or brooch back
Epoxy adhesive

## Tools:
Tile nippers
Safety goggles
Scissors
Small-nosed pliers
Cocktail stick
Small rolling pin
Craft knife
PVA glue
Oven
Baking tray

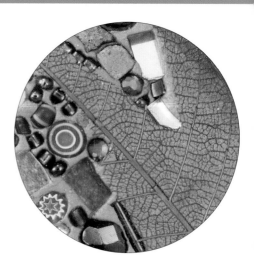

## Instructions:

**1** Roll out the modelling clay to about 3mm (1/8in). Lay one of the skeleton leaves over the clay and cut around the leaf shape with a craft knife. Set the excess clay aside. Using the scissors, cut a leaf-shaped hole in either side of the skeleton leaf to accommodate the decorative items.

**2** Dab a little glue on the clay and push the leaf shape into the clay gently using your fingers, and making sure it is stuck down and covers all of the clay neatly. You can trim more clay away from the edges with the craft knife to give it a precise edge.

**3** Using the cocktail stick, start pushing the beads and small pieces of tile and mirror into the clay through the holes that you have made on either side of the leaf. Add any other interesting pieces you may have such as millefiori, flat-backed crystals or gems. Avoid plastic gems as they could melt in the oven. Try to keep all the beads level with the clay and do not push them in so far that they look sunken.

**4** Cut a short length of silver wire and, using some small-nosed pliers, create some tiny swirls to press into the decorated area.

**5** Once you have completed the leaf and made a few others with different coloured modelling clay and beads, place them on a baking tray and put them in the oven for half an hour on 110°C/230°F/ gas mark ¼.

**6** Once cooled, they can be mounted on an attractive bathroom tile using epoxy adhesive. Apply a fixing on the back to hang using the same adhesive, as it is very strong and waterproof.

**7** Alternatively, the leaves can be used as jewellery – leave them unmounted and simply apply a brooch back.

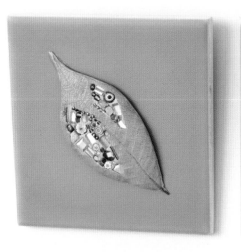

# Stone Pearls

## Materials:

MDF board approx. 9 x 9cm (3½ x 3½in)

Gold smalti

Red plaster tiles

Trimmings

Sequins

Millefiori

Craft sprinkles

Beads

Grout

Epoxy adhesive

Picture hook

Paint

## Tools:

Tile nippers

Safety goggles

Scissors

Paintbrush

Pencil

Cocktail stick

## Instructions:

**1** As the red tiles are made from plaster of Paris, it is easy to cut them with scissors if you do not have tile nippers. If you cannot find these tiles, it is fine to use stone or ceramic tiles instead.

**2** Using the pencil, draw some freehand curves down the board on either side, making an extended eye shape to create the flower garden section in the middle.

**3** Follow the pencil lines with the paintbrush and apply some glue. Start placing the gold smalti tiles one by one next to each other to frame the garden area first.

**4** Continue adding red plaster tiles behind the gold ones, following the curve next to the gold so that the tiles flow down the board. Using small triangular pieces makes it easy to form a curve within the design. Remember to leave spaces in between the tiles for the grout.

**5** Once the mosaic section is completed, leave it to dry for an hour, then grout it following the manufacturer's instructions, leaving the space for the garden area clear.

**6** To make the garden, apply the glue in small sections at a time and place down the

beads, sequins, flower gems, millefiori and trims. While the glue is still wet, sprinkle on the craft moss and use the cocktail stick to push it into the gaps.

**7** Once it is finished, leave it to dry and paint the edges. Attach a picture hook to the back using epoxy adhesive.

**Note:** For a different effect, use a natural stone colour for the tiles instead of the red or terracotta colour.

# Stone Rivers

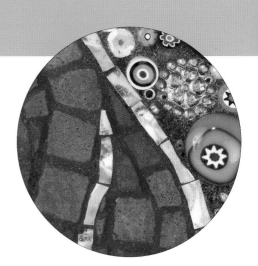

## Materials:

MDF board approx. 9 x 9cm
   (3½ x 3½in)
Gold smalti
Grey plaster tiles
Trimmings
Sequins
Millefiori
Craft moss sprinkles
Beads
Grout

Epoxy adhesive
Picture hook
Paint

## Tools:

Tile nippers
Safety goggles
Scissors
Paintbrush
Pencil
Cocktail stick

## Instructions:

**1** As the grey tiles are made from plaster of Paris, it is easy to cut them with scissors if you do not have tile nippers. If you cannot find these tiles, use stone or ceramic tiles instead.

**2** Using the pencil, draw some curves freehand down the board on either side, making a river shape to create the flower garden section in the middle.

**3** Follow the pencil lines with the paintbrush and apply some glue. Start placing the gold smalti tiles one by one next to each other to frame the garden area first.

**4** Continue adding grey plaster tiles behind the gold ones, following the curve next to the gold, so the tiles flow down the board. Using small triangular pieces makes it easy to form a curve within the design. Remember to leave spaces in between the tiles for the grout.

**5** Once the mosaic section is completed, leave it to dry for an hour, then grout it following the manufacturer's instructions, leaving the space for the garden area clear.

**6** To make the garden, apply the glue in small sections at a time and place down the beads, sequins, flower gems, millefiori and trims. While the glue is still wet, sprinkle on the craft moss and use the cocktail stick to push it into the gaps.

**7** Once it is finished, leave it to dry and paint the edges. Attach a picture hook to the back using epoxy adhesive.

**Note:** For a different effect, use a blue stone colour for the tiles instead of the grey colour.

# Cascade Necklace

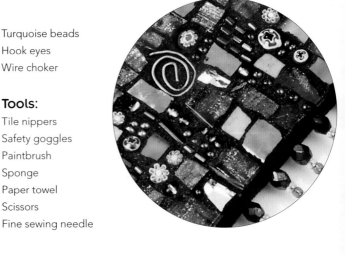

## Materials:

MDF board 7.5 x 5cm (3 x 2in)
PVA glue
Strong cotton thread
Wire
Millefiori
Mirror
Seed beads
Glass beads
Blue and grey glass tiles
Blue and grey ceramic tiles
Black grout

Turquoise beads
Hook eyes
Wire choker

## Tools:

Tile nippers
Safety goggles
Paintbrush
Sponge
Paper towel
Scissors
Fine sewing needle

## Instructions:

1 Cut up the strong thread with scissors into ten strips of 30.5cm (12in) each. Glue the board and lay out the ten threads, equally spaced, from the top of board so they will dangle down when beaded at a later stage.

2 With the tile nippers, cut up all the tiles in blues and greys and start laying them out on top of the board. Stick them down a section at a time, on top of the threads. Add millefiori, large beads and mirror pieces, leaving space for the grout and larger spaces for smaller beads that will go in once it is grouted.

3 When the mosaic is done, leave it for an hour or so or until the glue dries clear.

4 Make up the grout according to the manufacturer's instructions.

5 Grout the mosaic and wipe off any excess, then gently push the tiny seed beads into the large gaps you have left for this purpose.

6 Leave it to dry for an hour, then clean it up with a damp sponge, and buff with a dry paper towel.

7 Put some glue around the edge of the mosaic to seal the grout and stop any marks

going onto skin or clothing. When it has dried, it is time to start beading.

8 Using a fine sewing needle, start from left to right and thread the first piece of cotton. Choose the beads to complement the tones in the mosaic design and graduate the length of the threads so that the longest ones are in the middle of the beading.

9 Attach the screw hooks to the top of the wood base, and add rings to attach the choker.

10 Finally, paint the back of the mosaic.

# Fox

## Materials:

MDF board approx.
   12.5 x 12.5cm (5 x 5in)

Paint

Smalti

PVA glue

Glass beads

Picture hook

## Tools:

Tile nippers

Safety goggles

Paintbrush

Scissors

## Instructions:

**1** Paint the board a plain colour of your choice and leave it to dry.

**2** Use the fox template below and enlarge it to 200 per cent. Alternatively, source your own image and either photocopy it or print it out on plain paper.

**3** Cut out the shape of the fox face and glue it down onto the board. This method of making mosaics has been used for centuries, rather like painting by numbers, and it gives you a clear idea of colours and an accuracy with shaping.

**4** Study the shades used and choose colours to match. Using the tile nippers, start cutting up the smalti into small pieces and keep them in separate piles of colours. Make sure you wear safety goggles for this process. The smalti will shatter when cut, so be aware that the area you are working in will get messy.

**5** Using the paintbrush, apply glue to the paper image and glue down the smalti. Be generous with the glue as it dries clear, and you need to make sure the tiles will adhere properly, as this project will not be grouted. The smalti should be placed as close as possible to each other, so there are no gaps.

**6** As the image develops, be aware of the movement of the fox's fur, following the lines on the image to get the right direction of flow. For the fox's eyes, cut a bead in half with the nippers and glue each half down.

**7** Once the mosaic design is complete, leave it to dry and, using some black watered-down paint, apply it around the edge of the subject to create a shadow and give it a 3D effect.

**8** When the paint is dry, attach a picture hook to the back and hang.

*Fox template:
enlarge to 200 per cent*

# Owl

## Materials:

MDF board approx.
  12.5 x 12.5cm (5 x 5in)
Paint
Smalti
PVA glue
Glass beads
Picture hook

## Tools:

Tile nippers
Safety goggles
Paintbrush
Scissors

## Instructions:

**1** Paint the board a plain colour of your choice and leave it to dry.

**2** Use the owl template below and enlarge it to 200 per cent. Alternatively, source your own image and either photocopy it or print it out on plain paper.

**3** Cut out the shape of the owl face and glue it down onto the board. This method of making mosaics has been used for centuries, rather like painting by numbers, and it gives you a clear idea of colours and an accuracy with shaping.

**4** Study the shades used and choose colours to match. Using the tile nippers, start cutting up the smalti into small pieces and keep them in separate piles of colours. Make sure you wear the safety goggles for this process. The smalti will shatter when cut, so be aware that the area you are working in will get messy.

**5** Using the paintbrush, apply glue to the paper image and glue down the smalti. Be generous with the glue as it dries clear, and you need to make sure the tiles will adhere properly, as this project will not be grouted. The smalti should be placed as close as possible to each other, so there are no gaps.

**6** As the image develops, be aware of the movement of the owl's feathers, following the lines on the image to get the right direction of flow. For the owl's eyes, cut a bead in half with the nippers and glue each half down.

**7** Once the mosaic design is complete, leave it to dry and, using some black watered-down paint, apply it around the edge of the subject to create a shadow and give it a 3D effect.

**8** When the paint is dry, attach a picture hook to the back and hang.

*Owl template:*
*enlarge to 200 per cent*

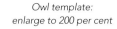

# Klimt Abstract

## Materials:

MDF board approx.
  8.5 x 15cm (3¾ x 6in)

Black paint

PVA glue

Mirror pieces

Millefiori

Shaped glass nuggets

Glass tiles

Ceramic tiles

Glass fusion

Beads

Picture hook

## Tools:

Tile nippers

Safety goggles

Paintbrush

Pencil

## Instructions:

**1** Start by painting the top and sides of the board black. As this project uses smalti, which are very uneven tiles, it will be not be grouted, so the paint helps to give it a more unified appearance. The idea for this project is to allow all the different materials to flow by placing them very closely together on the board. Using a special stone or glass fusion as a focal point, glue that on in the centre first. Glass fusions are beautiful to work with and, as they are normally made as a one-off, they lend the work a unique quality.

**2** Next, draw a swirl or two around the glass fusion, as lines to follow. Apply some glue along the lines quite generously, as it will help to stick down the uneven pieces of smalti, which should be placed on their sides.

**3** Keep the materials in little colour groups so that you can graduate the tones from light to dark and keep the lines of mosaic tiles in a flowing shape, aided by the colours. As the shapes of the pieces change, getting wider or narrower, you can add small beads to the tiny gaps.

**4** Work your way up the board changing the tones of the colours as you go, and adding beads, millefiori and sequins. Make a swirl of golds and yellows, or another colour of your choice, around the glass fusion to create some flow and emphasis within the shades of green.

**5** Leave the design to dry for an hour or so.

**6** Attach a picture hook to the back and hang.

# Ancient Gardens

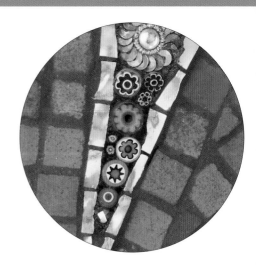

**Materials:**

MDF board approx. 13 x 36cm
(5 x 14½in)

Gold smalti

Red plaster tiles

Trims

Sequins

Millefiori

Craft sprinkles

Beads

Grout

Epoxy adhesive

Picture hook

Paint

**Tools:**

Tile nippers

Safety goggles

Scissors

Paintbrush

Pencil

Cocktail stick

## Instructions:

**1** As the red tiles are made from plaster of Paris, it is easy to cut them with scissors if you do not have tile nippers. If you cannot find these tiles, use stone or ceramic tiles instead.

**2** Using the pencil, draw some long curves freehand down the board on either side, making a traingular shape at the top to create the flower garden section.

**3** Follow the pencil lines with the paintbrush and apply some glue. Start placing the gold smalti tiles next to each other, one by one, to frame the garden area and create the long curve down to the bottom of the board.

**4** Continue adding red plaster tiles behind the gold ones, following the curve next to the gold, so it flows down the board. Using small triangular pieces makes it easy to form

a curve within the design. Remember to leave spaces in between the tiles for the grout.

**5** Once the mosaic section is completed, leave it to dry for an hour, then grout it following the manufacturer's instructions, leaving the space for the garden area clear.

**6** To make the garden, apply the glue in small sections at a time and place down the beads, sequins, flower gems, millefiori and trims. While the glue is still wet, sprinkle on the craft moss and use the cocktail stick to push it into the gaps.

**7** Once it is finished, leave it to dry and paint the edges. Attach a picture hook to the back using epoxy adhesive.

# Fish Plate

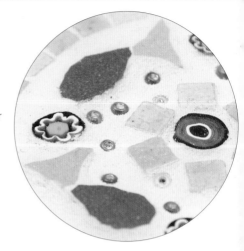

## Materials:

Side plate

PVA glue

Silicone adhesive

Blue and yellow ceramic tiles

Mini tiles in greeny-blue shades

Millefiori

Glass beads

Seed beads

Beige grout

Plate hanger

## Tools:

Tile nippers

Safety goggles

Paintbrush

Cocktail stick

Wooden coffee stirrer

Cloth or paper towel

## Instructions:

**1** Using a ruler, find the centre of the side plate and stick down the millefiori as a centrepiece, with a little dab of silicone adhesive applied using the cocktail stick.

**2** Start cutting out the little blue fish shapes. The body of the fish starts as a 2cm (¾in) rectangle and the edges are nibbled off to form the body; the little tail is a square cut diagonally to create a triangle. Place them dry in the circle to see how many will fit evenly in the area of the centrepiece.

**3** Using the wooden coffee stirrer, start gluing down the fish, one by one. Work on the centre design, adding four more millefiori and yellow fish swimming in the opposite direction to the blue fish.

**4** Leave to dry for an hour.

**5** The mosaic mini tiles are glued down on the flat part of the plate next using the PVA glue and the paintbrush,

Apply the glue directly to the plate and stick down evenly and neatly, following the line and shape of the plate.

**6** Next, stick the mini tiles on the sloping part of the plate. The silicone adhesive is very useful, as it will hold the tiles down without them sliding away.

**7** There will be a considerable amount of space around the fish and the mosaic tiles – this is fine, as the grout will fill the gaps perfectly.

**8** Leave the whole plate to dry for at least two hours or more before grouting.

**9** Make up the grout following the manufacturer's instructions, and grout the mosaic mini tiles area first. Clean it up with a dry paper towel, then spread the remaining grout over the fish area evenly, cleaning it up as much as possible with more dry paper towel. Once it is

clean, use the cocktail stick to push in the seed beads and little glass beads around the outside edge of the fish, but this must be done quite quickly as the grout hardens as it is drying and the beads are not so easy to push in.

**10** Leave it to dry for an hour.

**11** Buff with a strong paper towel or damp cloth.

**12** Seal with a solution of one part water and two parts PVA glue to create a varnish to stop the grout from crumbling. Brush this all over the plate and leave to dry completely.

**13** Hang using a plate hanger from a craft store.

For more information you
are invited to visit the
author's website:
www.mosaicmadromans.com

## Acknowledgements

My special thanks to Meera from Aarti J, who inspired me with her beautiful trimmings,
beads and sequins, and to the Venice Simplon-Orient-Express for the opportunity to nurture
their ageing mosaics. Thank you to my children, Barney, Cloe, and Greg for living with a
workaholic mother, to my mother Susan Searle for support and strength; and gratitude to my
good friends Alex, Theresa, Nikki, Katherine and David who have been there alongside me,
encouraging me. I love you all. But the biggest thanks for making this, my first book,
happen is to May Corfield and the team at Search Press. Thank you!